Zebras
Stop Looking for

Robert B. Smith RGD

Zeb

Stop Looking for ras

Observations, essays, and rants to help you experience a long and fulfilling creative career.

Copyright © 2023 Robert B. Smith

All rights reserved. No part of this publication may be reproduced, distributed, or transmitted in any form or by any means, including photocopying, recording, or other electronic or mechanical methods, without the prior written permission of the publisher, except in the case of brief quotations embodied in critical reviews and certain other noncommercial uses permitted by copyright law. For permission requests, write to the author, addressed "Attention: Permissions " at robert@think-smith.com.

First Edition

ISBN: 978-1-7751701-3-6 (print)
ISBN: 978-1-7751701-4-3 (ebook)

Design: Robert B. Smith

Editor: Valerie Boucher

Illustrations: Chelle Lorenzen
www.heychelle.com

Typeset in Minion Pro

Freshly Pressed/Think-Smith
Ottawa, Ontario
Canada K2J 2T3

Ordering Information:
robert@think-smith.com

www.think-smith.com

Acknowledgments

This book is dedicated to my dad.
Here is the book that I was telling you about.
I wish you were here to read it.

All illustrations by Chelle Lorenzen.
You brought the illustrative wit, sass and attitude that this project needed.
heychelle.com

A sincere thank you to all of those who endured this process with me. It would not have happened without you. I am truly blessed to have such wonderful people around me. In no particular order:

Mom (Susan), Zack, Nathan, Kim, Erica & Wayne, Russel, Luc, Jess, Kiara, Val, Chelle, Carol, Philip, Heather & Jeff, Mike, Jill, Mark, Michelle, Jenny, Richard & Carol, my TEC group and EVERYONE at the RGD.

Finally, to all of my amazing friends and family, online and offline, you make me smile everyday and I love you for it.

life doesn't come with

a table of contents

And neither does this book. You can pick it up at any point. You can even start at the end. So, let's explore how to present concepts like a family dinner; what an Olympian can teach us about focus; how not to be a tool and why vacuum cleaners are not a creative strategy.

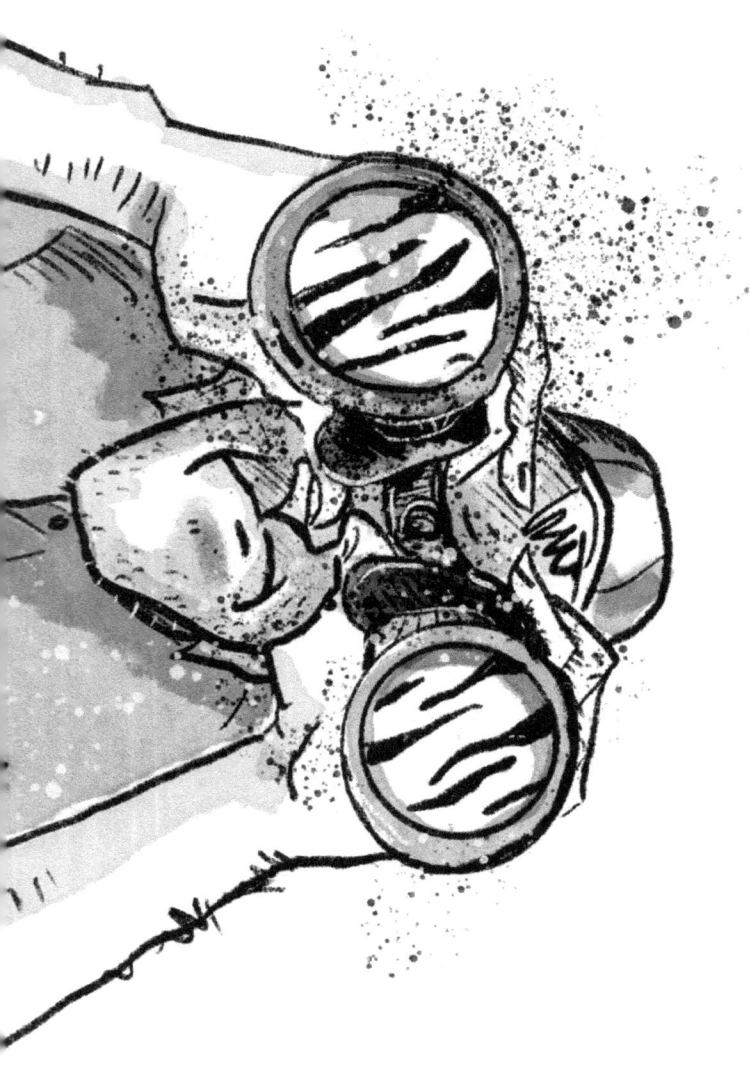

I see you.

Worrying. Wandering. Wondering.

You've got a diploma and *worrying* about what's next? Maybe you're halfway through your career and it feels like you have been *wandering* with nothing much to show for it. Or a late career creative who is *wondering* if it was worth all the hours and dedication? If, after all these years, you've made an impact.

I see you because ***I am you.***

"oh, the thinks you will think."

— Dr. Seuss

This book is not a: textbook, how-to, idiot's guide, manifesto, fiction, portfolio, instruction manual, diary, script, "bible", diet plan, get rich quick scheme, fairy tale, fable, folklore, or bedtime story.

This book **is** a conversation.

Introduction

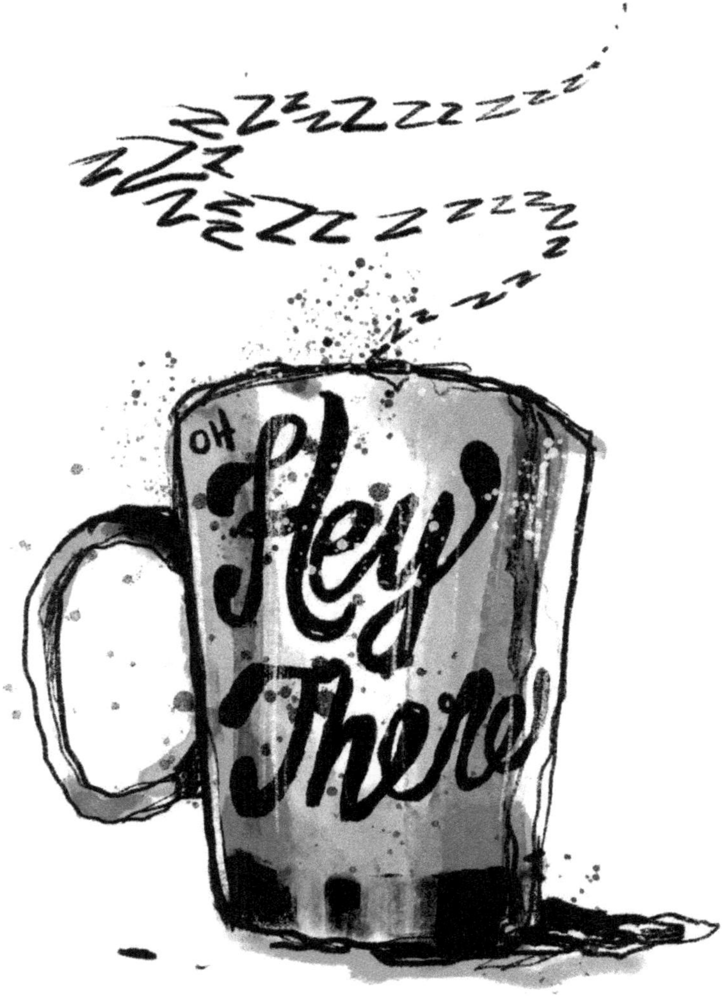
OH
Hey
There

Hey there!

I need you to be completely honest with me, and yourself, right now. Don't worry, it's just the two of us (we'll get to who I am in a minute).

At this moment in your life, are you doing what you love? Are you fulfilled and living your best creative life? Are you struggling?

Don't yell out the answer (that would be weird). I am going to go ahead and guess that you are not. Well, at least not to your full potential or there is room for improvement. I can also assume you are reading this book because you're either looking for answers or are intrigued by the title (or you're my mother).

The good news is, this means you are at least a little bit curious. There is no trait better than curiosity.

When you are curious, life is an adventure. Like a child, you can greet the day with enthusiasm and energy. What will this day bring? What will I learn? Let's be honest though, not every day is like that. The struggle can be very real. We can reduce the number of "those" days if we truly want to, though. This book provides some of my observations gathered over a 30-year career. And trust me I have seen a lot and I am far from done.

Also, this book is not about getting a six or seven figure salary, but it may help.

Ultimately, I want you to wake up every morning appreciating the clients you have and work ahead. No coffee, alcohol, sugar or other stimulus required.

I have been in this industry long enough to have experienced most of what you are going through and have either, failed, excelled or mostly shook my head. I wrote this book because I know the struggles and frustrations that you are or will be facing. I am, however, not psychic. Frustrating but true, so I have put together these essays, observations and rants to help you regain your creative power, and sanity.

I have been in this industry long enough to have experienced most of what you are going through and have either, excelled, failed, or simply shook my head.

So, who is this guy?

(Not that) Robert Smith

Let me start by saying that I am NOT the lead singer of The Cure, an '80s band that you will be familiar with if you are of a certain age, or have good taste (if not ask your parents). This Robert Smith is a dad, professor, business owner, creative director and author. Instead of playing hockey or other sports, I am a mediocre drummer in a band with some buddies.

I have worked for a government department, large corporation, small agencies and started two of my own. I am a professor and a founder of the Association of Registered Designers.

My work has appeared in over 100 publications including *Communication Arts, Applied Arts, Graphis,* and *Critique* among others. I have also been honored to take the stage as a speaker at design conferences and hosted many workshops and webinars.

I am blessed, but it wasn't always that way.

High School Heartbreak

It's not what you think. We all experience heartbreak in high school. That one person that captured our imagination. Made math class a joy by their very presence. I certainly had that experience more often than I would like to admit but this is deeper. It was the heartbreak of self.

High school had broken me. My self-esteem bottomed out and I was lost. I graduated with bare-bottom grades and no direction. As an artistic teenager, I didn't seem to fit in academically and it translated to my self-worth. Shitty and wrong. Hindsight is twenty-twenty, as we know, and I now look back and see that there was a path for me. A wonderful and exciting path.

In my final year of high school, I was blessed with the wisdom of an incredible guidance counselor. Aware of my drawing abilities and thought patterns, he suggested that I go into graphic design. Fantastic! What's graphic design? After walking me through several books of graphic design showing me examples it was that iconic light bulb moment, this is a job!?!

I then went onto three years of college in graphic design, was vice-president of the student body and awarded the president's list when I graduated.

I'm here now to tell you that there's a path for each and every one of you and it's a good one. It's fun, it's challenging, it's nerve-wracking even heartbreaking, but ultimately it is fulfilling.

I've been in the industry for close to 30 years. I've worked for a government department, an international corporation, owned two agencies and I've been teaching senior college students about creativity for over 10 years.

Thirty years. Wow. Can you imagine being in the same industry for 30 years and still waking up most mornings energized and inspired? There is certainly no way I would have guessed that would be me.

After 30 years in the creative industry I can honestly say that I am still inspired, driven and energized.

I want the same for you.

Let me guess, y
"disruptive" as a
rouser, up to no
on you! Wait, w
client has just a
disruptive?

ou were labeled
 child. A rabble
 good. Shame
hat's that? Your
sked you to be

"It was the best of times, it was the worst of times, it was the age of wisdom, it was the age of foolishness. We had everything before us, we had nothing before us."

— Charles Dickens, *A Tale of Two Cities*

Creativity
and the French Revolution

So, what does the French Revolution have to do with creativity and communications? Nothing really, but the quote on the previous page has stuck with me over the years. It's the beginning of Charles Dickens' *A Tale of Two Cities*, a fictional account of the French Revolution. To me, this quote also applies to the current state of our industry.

Let's break it down.

"It was the best of times, it was the worst of times, it was the age of wisdom, it was the age of foolishness. We had everything before us, we had nothing before us."

For visual communicators, "it's the best of times" because society in general, is looking for better. Better design, better content, better work. It has become an endless hunger, fed through social media and digital engagement. This has translated into more jobs, opportunities and, in some cases, better salaries.

It's "the worst of times" because everyone is a content expert. We all have access to a seemingly endless buffet of fonts, templates and stock images. Let's be honest, a lot of them are beautiful but are they what the client needs? We now find ourselves not only competing with other professionals but also with the easy and cheap, ready-to-go templates. Basically drive-through solutions. Do you want fries with that?

"It was the best of times, it was the worst of times, *it was the age of wisdom, it was the age of foolishness.* We had everything before us, we had nothing before us."

We are trapped in a conundrum. On one hand, we need to be an expert. Audiences are looking for insight, advice and thought leadership. Wisdom. The pressure is high to deliver engaging content for ourselves and our clients. Constantly. The fact that the creative process hasn't changed but the demand increased ten-fold is daunting.

The volume of imagery that is bombarding everyone on a daily, and hourly basis is astounding and only getting worse. At the risk of sounding like a grumpy old man, I feel the "foolishness" in this quote can be seen as viral videos and repeated platitudes that seem to never end. It's a competitive time where anyone with a smartphone can create content. That doesn't guarantee it's any good, but it adds to the noise anyway. Everyone is drawn to them like flies to a light bulb. A roadside attraction. Does it communicate? Not really, but it has an audience and that cannot be denied or ignored.

"It was the best of times, it was the worst of times, it was the age of wisdom, it was the age of foolishness. We had everything before us, we had nothing before us."

We certainly have everything before us. Opportunities for communicators in the design, writing, photography, and video industries have increased with the demand for content. More and more jobs are opening up in a vast number of industries. Almost too many. It can be overwhelming if you don't know what you want.

That said, it won't just appear. Like in the quote, there is "nothing before us" if you wait for it to happen. You have to work at it. There is a lot of noise out there and you need to be heard. You need to educate your clients and demonstrate the value that you bring. Delivering a return on investment, ROI, is more important than ever.

> "Even if you're on the right track, you'll get run over if you just sit there."
>
> — Will Rogers

Career

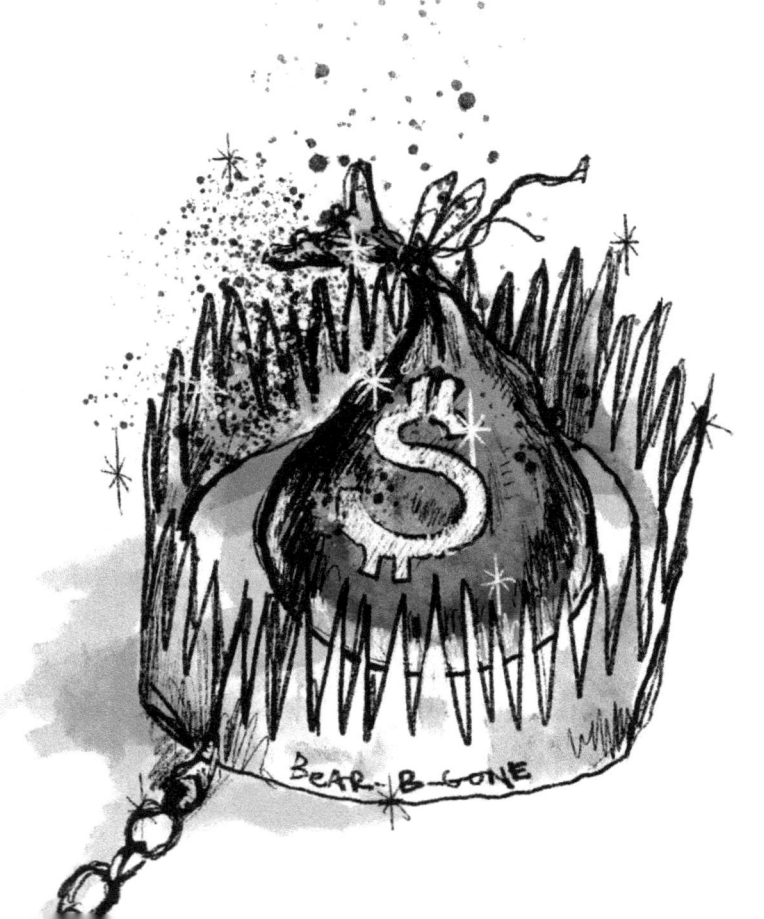

Goals
and Bear Traps

Dissatisfaction in the workplace is one of the most stressful situations you can find yourself in. You don't want to get up in the morning. You hit the snooze button like you're playing "whack-a-mole". There's suddenly not enough coffee in the world to take off the edge. How did you get into this situation? Like aimlessly walking through the forest and suddenly BAM you step in a bear trap. Where the hell did that come from? How did you not see it there? Damn it hurts and you can't move.

Are you stuck?

For some the bear trap is financial, for others security, rigid structure. The truth is, if we don't pay attention and aimlessly wander without a map we will end up lost.

Maybe you took a job because it pays well and your lifestyle depends on it, but it isn't inspiring. It isn't enjoyable.

Maybe your job isn't moving the way you hoped it would.

Maybe you're struggling to find creative work in general.

"I'm Losing My Soul"

That was the case for a former student of mine who reached out to me. It had been five years since she graduated and she was stuck. She said she's losing her soul and needs to get creative again. Right out of school she took the first job that she found. It offered everything, or so she thought. Predictable hours, benefits, breaks, multiple weeks of vacation and most importantly, it thrilled her parents. What's more important, the lifestyle or piece of mind job? She was in a bear trap.

Avoiding Bear Traps

Being present is the key to ensuring that you don't stray from your path or as some call it "your lane". If you are simply walking through the woods, looking at the trees and not paying attention, you will surely trip on a branch, stumble on a rock or step into a bear trap. It is inevitable. If, however, you look down occasionally and pay attention to your steps you will get to where you are going without becoming stuck or ending up in the ER. Your career is the same.

If you keep walking without intention, you will eventually stop and wonder, how did I get here?

This rings true for many of us. Experiencing an existential crisis after acquiring all of the expected achievements and things that we are told are important. Ask yourself: are they?

There are no wrong answers.

Your Career
and the Frog in a Pot

Another way to look at your career is the story about the frog in a pot. There doesn't seem to be any scientific proof of this but it serves as a great metaphor for job satisfaction.

Essentially, a frog is put into boiling water (don't actually do this!). Feeling the danger, it will immediately jump out to safety. If, however, the same frog is put into a pot of lukewarm water, and the temperature is slowly increased, it will not perceive any danger and will be cooked to death.

Gross! I know, but why would it allow that to happen?

Because the frog is only slightly uncomfortable as the heat increases, it will simply adjust and get accustomed to the new temperature. Swimming around, it eventually tires and can't jump out when the water reaches a dangerous temperature.

A lot of people find themselves in an employment situation that is not satisfying, is challenging or even toxic. Why do they stay? The quick answer is routine and familiarity. We don't like change so we put up with bad situations. And the bullshit!

Like the frog, you can easily find yourself five, even 10 or more years in a situation that has progressively eaten away at your creativity, drive, and will to get up in the morning. You may have moved positions, offices or even buildings but the overall situation has not changed.

It's important to stop every now and then and see where you are. Is it what you want? Are you happy?

Is the water boiling?

The Five Stages of (Career) Grief

Buzz…Buzz…Buzz…SMACK!
Please, just five more minutes.

It's 9:30 a.m. and you're sitting at your desk thinking if you hear Brad's raspy cackle one more time you are going to throw your mug at his big balding head.

You need more coffee…but, what's the issue? Is it you? The job? Brad?

In 1969, Swiss psychiatrist Elisabeth Kübler-Ross published her book *On Death and Dying*. In it, she defines the five stages of grief as: denial, anger, bargaining, depression and acceptance. These can also be applied to one's career.

You may recognize some of these when you think about your own work situation.

You may, for example, feel trapped or unfulfilled making you angry or depressed. You may have given up and accepted where you are, thinking that you can't make a change. These stages are outlined here for you to identify where you may be. The point is to take action and not stay in the stage that you find yourself in.

Here are the 5 stages of career grief and how to identify them. Unlike Elisabeth Kübler-Ross's stages, these are not necessarily sequential.

Stage 1
Denial

Denial can take two forms. The first is denying that there is a problem. You landed the job everyone said was perfect for you. Your parents couldn't be happier. Even though you are unhappy, you convince yourself otherwise. You have to be happy, right? Everyone says so.

Well, if you are working a job you hate or have chosen a career that isn't fulfilling then you need to stop denying your own feelings. Stop listening to everyone else and start looking inward. You spend way too much time at work to settle. The result will be resentment. If this sounds familiar, you will certainly move to Stage 2, anger. If you push through denial into awareness then you can save yourself from all of the other stages of Career Grief and skip forward to Stage 3, resolution.

Stage 2
ANG

Your dissatisfaction has hit the boiling point. From someone who sat quietly mumbling at your desk by yourself, you have become toxic. People avoid you. Your work suffers, your colleagues suffer, your family suffers and your poor alarm clock sits in the corner of your bedroom in a disjointed pile of plastic. More importantly, you suffer.

The stress and anxiety has boiled over and it is masked in anger. So now what? Well, if you are acknowledging the fact that you are angry that's the first step. Now, identify the problem. Is it salary, a promotion, recognition or do you want a desk closer to the coffee machine?

ER!!!

Anger should be recognized and be followed up with a nice cup of reflection (and a shot of calm the hell down!).

Recognizing that you are going to work feeling negative and angry is actually beneficial. It means that you are aware of your situation and can now reflect and move onto Stage 3 with a better perspective. If you jump straight from anger to bargaining without reflection, you will fail.

There is rarely a plan when you react in anger, so go back to the beginning of Stage 2 and stop being an ass. AND STOP DRINKING COFFEE! Maybe try some herbal tea.

Stage 3
Negotiation &

Welcome to Stage 3! This is where we flip the 5 stages of grief. Instead of slowly moving from stage to stage in dealing with grief, in career grief Stage 3 is the goal. Stage 4 and 5 are the results of inaction.

Stage 3 is about empowerment. You now know what you want and you must take action. This is also where the wheels fall off if you jump to Stage 3 prematurely. Like I said at the end of Stage 2, reacting with anger will almost always have negative results.

Some people will jump to the conclusion that the only option is to quit. Quitting is only if you have tried everything else.

Resolution

Your first action should be to fix where you are. If you have a clear idea of what you want, present it to your employer. You have nothing to lose. You are already unhappy. Don't forget that there is a great deal of stress associated with looking for or starting a new job. Your best action here is to try fixing where you are. Book a meeting with your boss, manager or HR. Talk it out. They are not psychic and may not know how you are feeling or what you need. Don't wait. Do it now!

Resolution is at hand. Now that you know what you want, you are ready to address it. Take action.

Stage 4
Depression

So, you're at Stage 4. Either you dealt with the situation and it didn't go your way or you have buried your head in the sand. It is the result of inaction or worse, Stage 5. These last two stages are interchangeable.

Stage 5
Acceptance

This stage should actually be called "giving up". Are you not paying attention? How have you made it to Stage 5? You need more than a hug, you need a kick in the ass.

You are basically back at Stage 1 without the deniability.

See how this is a loop. Your penance here is to go back to Stage 1 and keep reading these over and over until Stage 3 sticks!

For some this process will work right away, for others it will take more work. Don't worry if you get to depression and or acceptance. A lot of people do. Just promise me you will start at the beginning and get back on track. It will likely involve buying another alarm clock, though.

Have You

Become Tragically Competent?

Are you too comfortable? Making things good enough? Living in a world where nothing is necessarily wrong but there is nothing right either. If this sounds like you, you have become 'Tragically Competent'. Over time, this will kill your spirit and while you will generally feel okay, there is an underlying unhappiness. You will, if not already, become unfulfilled and start to feel bitter about how you've spent your time and regret what you didn't pursue.

Competent is dangerous and expensive.

Competent work is neither good nor bad and that is the problem. It will not offend anyone but it will not inspire or interest anyone either. Even bad work gets noticed for being, well, bad.

Don't fool yourself. Being tragically competent is not lazy or safe. It's actually very scary. And risky. And expensive! As I've said before even bad ideas get noticed, but not being noticed is a scary situation.

It's not a sound strategy for increasing revenues, gaining a bigger audience or personal growth. It's simply maintaining. If we compare this to something medical it's basically a flat line. Which is dead.

Why tragic?

Simply put, this is a privileged career. NEVER take it for granted. It is absolutely tragic if you are simply going through the motions and taking this career for granted. I can't say it strongly enough.

I was fortunate enough to work in a warehouse for two summers to pay for school. The full-time staff were jaded and angry most days. Monday was the worst day of the week and Friday the best. The rest were a dull buzz of clock watching and complaining. My greatest lesson was that I never wanted to be in that situation again.

The creative industry provides us with the opportunity to continually learn. In order to do our job well, we need to immerse ourselves in our client's business, their customers/clients and the industry they compete in.

At this point I count myself very fortunate to know how a craft brewery operates, how artisan cheese is made, what a metro optical network is and to have been behind the scenes at a few trendy restaurants.

It is absolutely tragic if you are simply going through the motions and taking this career for granted.

Paging Dr. Smith...

A number of years ago I was asked by our local hospital to help them raise a substantial amount of funds for their desperately needed expansion. Their targets were individuals and corporations that would donate $500k and above.

To me this meant that we needed to do something impactful. Special. Aside from the writing and design, I was adamant that we not use stock photography. This piece had to be genuine, real and urgent. My client contacted me the next day. "Careful what you wish for," she warned.

One week later I was changing into scrubs and spending an entire shift at the hospital. We were only allowed minimal camera equipment and no lighting. For the next 8 hours I was in the ER, OR, ICU, ambulance and birthing unit. My shift was enlightening, exhausting and life-changing. We ended up with incredibly real imagery, a compelling message and a deep appreciation of what our healthcare workers deal with on a daily basis.

At the end of my "shift" I was changing and a surgeon came in to prepare for his day. He looked over at my bent-over exhaustion and commented "busy day?" "Six surgeries, a birth and three emergencies." He threw a confused look my way. "Well, I took pictures, I didn't do the work."

This experience is something that I will never forget and only happened because I asked.

Will you get to do a shift in a hospital? Maybe not, but the opportunities are there.

How Free is Your Freelancing?

Freelance is such a loaded word in our industry. It can be met with positivity, indifference and even disdain. How can this be when it's how so many of us start our career? We will take any work we can get in order to gain experience and build our portfolio. Then it becomes a side hustle and sometimes matures into a business. There is a line though when you are freelancing while an employee. That is where the friction happens and you need to make a decision.

We transition from drawing in class to band posters, wedding invitations and birth announcements. It becomes a part of our life. After school and then after work, we sit in front of a screen or sketchpad and apply our creativity.

Left unchecked, it can take up a lot of our time and the compensation is not equal to the effort. What started as a hobby has become an expensive use of our time. Underpaid and frustrated, you can easily become disenchanted and disengaged.

You are basically in a state of indecision. Limbo. If you are gainfully employed and freelancing you need to stop and ask yourself why.

If you are gainfully employed AND freelancing you need to stop and ask yourself why.

Part-time
Freelancer

The Side Hustle

You're working full-time but not fulfilled either financially or creatively. After spending a full day at work you head home for another "shift". Back to the drawing board, sketch pad or computer. Another client, project, deadline and pot of coffee.

The first question you must ask yourself is if you're freelancing for the money. If this is to offset your current salary then I would suggest you either:

a) ask for a raise
b) find a new job that pays better
c) adjust your lifestyle.

The Portfolio Builder

If you're doing it to build out your portfolio, that is an acceptable strategy. Do you really need a client for this or can you simply "re-imagine" a brand or project? Fill a hole in your portfolio with a self-directed project. It will give you the experience without the business headache. Better yet, find a charity or not-for-profit. There are so many deserving associations and groups who simply don't have the funds but desperately need the help.

Full-time
Freelancer

This is how most agencies start. Both of mine were started as freelancing from my home.

If you are doing this full-time, then you need to stop calling it freelancing. WHAT?!?! Yes, I said it. Here's why: you are a business and calling yourself a freelancer can impact your ability to charge more for your work. Semantics? Maybe, but language is powerful and perception is reality. If you want to be treated seriously and charge a good rate, you are a business. You will also take it seriously in your head. Freelancing, the term, can feel non-committal.

Don't get me wrong, part-time freelancing is a business as well, but not at the same level.

The Strategies

You have two paths ahead of you if you choose to do this full-time. Each has a very different tactic to it and promotional approach.

Option 1
The Hired Gun

Your strategy is to approach larger agencies as a hired gun. You're a commando dropped into the agency as a specialist to get things done when they are busy. Agencies rely on freelancers to help out when work goes beyond their area of expertise or they simply have too much work.

In this case you should brand and promote yourself under your own name. Many designers go straight to building a brand and company name when they decide to go full-time. If you are targeting agencies, this can prove problematic. Agencies hire an individual to help them out, not a company.

The Upside

a) You may not have to deal with the client. Client services can eat up a lot of time.

b) You will not have to chase clients down for payment, just the agency.

c) There is an opportunity to collaborate. Working on your own can be lonely.

The Downside

a) You will be invisible to the client.

b) Your work will be marked up, so your fee potential will likely have a ceiling.

c) You will likely not be able to put the work in your portfolio.

Option 2
The Company

You are seeking out clients who require your services directly. There is no studio buffer here. You are directly working with business clients. Certainly empowering and potentially more lucrative but also represents more time and effort on your part.

You will not have the insulation of account managers, production managers, client liaisons etcetera. You are all of these things, assuming that you do not have staff.

The Upside

a) You will have control over the work that comes in.

b) All fees go to you. You will have more earning potential as there will be no mark-up of your services.

c) You will be able to put the work in your portfolio.

The Downside

a) You deal with the client directly. Client services can eat up a lot of time.

b) You will have to chase clients down for payment.

c) There is less opportunity to collaborate. Working on your own can be lonely.

If it isn't making money, it's an expensive hobby.

One of the problems of freelancing is clients will expect to pay a fraction of your value. This is a myth perpetuated by the availability of low-cost templated solutions, people with rudimentary design skills learned on YouTube or simply hacking their way through it. How hard can it be, right? The fact that you are reading this means that you have taken this career more seriously.

Your freelance business is just that, a business. If you aren't making money, then it's a hobby. When you treat it like a business then others will.

Invest in Yourself

A Freelance Alternative

We can reach a point where we spend all our working hours (and beyond) making money for other people. Promoting their products, creating brands and writing ad copy. While all of this is quite fulfilling, it's not entirely feeding the soul. We still have that creative side and inner child that wants to draw.

Consider taking this time to make money for yourself. Launch that product idea. Explore ideas that you may have had for new product whether by software, physical or service. Work for a charity. Learn a musical instrument. All of these things will help your creativity. Maybe there was something that you used to do that lead you to designing and writing. If you're a writer, write that book, short story or poems. If you're a designer that came to the profession from an interest in fine art then explore that. Paint, draw, film and photograph. Unabashedly explore your creative side. Invest in yourself.

You Are Not Psychic

I know this will come as a great disappointment but you are not psychic. You never have been and you never will be. So, stop assuming things are going to go a certain way or a person is going to react a certain way. Give the situation the opportunity to happen. Remember that the only thing you're in control of is yourself and your own reactions, not anybody else's.

The Core Cause of Impostor Syndrome

Do these statements sound familiar?

- *The client will never accept that.*
- *I can't possibly charge that much.*
- *That will never get approved.*
- *Will the client think my work is worth the cost?*
- *What if they hate it?*
- *There are so many people better than me.*

It's easy to fall into a trap of putting down your own abilities.

How does this affect creativity? Are you kidding me? It is one of the main blocks in getting things done. It is at the core of Impostor Syndrome.

Impostor Syndrome is the single most common cause of creative paralysis. It's the asshole in your head telling you that you are not good enough, your concept is stupid, you will never be able to fix this etc… Sound familiar? The key to understanding Impostor Syndrome is that the majority of the thinking is associated with assumptions about the future. "The client will never approve that". Won't they? How do you know? "That is a stupid idea" Is it? Based on what? Again, these are assumptions. What is key here is that we have not given the client the chance to shoot it down. We haven't considered anything except for our own inner asshole chirping in our ear. Take the emotion out of it. Look at the creative brief. Consult your research. The answers are there and if you have considered everything provided to you, it is good to present. After all, this is preliminary and will require revisions and refinements. So show your sketches, your rough ideas. You are not psychic and cannot possibly know what the reaction will be. Confidence will come from the acknowledgment that you have checked all of the boxes in the brief.

…SO, GET OUT OF YOUR OWN WAY.

All these thoughts are entrenched in self-doubt. Not data. It's easy to assume the worst and project fears before you even get started.

My own self doubt has been a constant struggle. I found myself in my 40's with a boat load of awards and accolades. The recognition of my colleagues and industry. I was speaking at conferences and asked to judge national and international design competitions. I was on top of the world or so it seemed.

An enviable career for sure. So why was I struggling to pay bills? I was constantly in debt and couldn't understand why, with all of this success, I couldn't afford simple things? Former students were eclipsing me in salary and lifestyle.

Self-doubt and impostor syndrome kept me from asking or expecting what my time was worth. I undercharged because I failed to see the value that I brought to the table. Insecurity drove me to enter competitions and seek out recognition, but I would not allow me to translate the "success" into personal wealth. Because I have been mainly self-employed, I didn't have the internal infrastructure to monitor my salary, apply raises and manage the financial needs of inflation. I hate math and it showed. I was in my own way and it was destructive. I couldn't blame bad clients, the economy or competition.

Insecurity drove me to enter design competitions and seek out recognition. I would not allow myself to translate the "success" into personal wealth.

Get Out of Your Own Way

The first step to building any kind of creative career is getting out of your own way and pushing past your self-doubt.

Get to know that voice of self-doubt and listen to how ridiculous it is. Once you do, you can start to quiet it.

It's all about being self-aware and paying attention. Your skills of observation are the silver bullet. Just like sunlight to a vampire, awareness will destroy some of these fears.

Can you remember a moment when things weren't actually as bad as you thought they were? Of course you can, we all can. We have the ability to blow things out of proportion and overreact. Just like recognizing our inner monster, seeing our fear for what it is will help you deal with it.

For example, I used to be deathly afraid of flying. No matter what people told me or the safety statistics put in front of me, it was something I passionately avoided. When I did have to fly it was a white-knuckled, eyes closed roller coaster until we landed (and this doesn't even include the weeks of heavy anxiety leading up to the flight). It was paralyzing and kept me from enjoying some of the fantastic places I have now visited.

My fear was addressed by simply rethinking the experience. Instead of focusing on the time in the air, I focused on my destination. The excitement of being in Mexico, New Orleans or Paris overpowered my fear. I replaced my pain and fear of flying, with pleasure, tequila and tacos! Nothing else changed, just my perspective. Your mind is incredibly powerful. As I said at the beginning, it can be your worst enemy but also your greatest power. It's all about perspective.

To reiterate: you are the scariest thing in your life. You scare the shit out of yourself. Probably daily! This fear works like a magnifier. Any situation will appear ten times worse through our eyes. My point is don't worry about something until there is something to worry about. Sounds silly but it is so true.

So, sit back, fasten your seatbelt and enjoy your flight. The destination is so worth it!

Bryan

Adams
Hasn't Heard of You Either

A Lesson in Tenacity

In the spring of 1981, a young Bryan Adams went into the studio to record his second album. His self-titled first album failed to chart and he was faced with the potential of being dropped by his record label.

After years of touring, songwriting and dedication, he had little to show for it. Now what?

Frustrated, but not down, he used this as an opportunity to work on new material and refocus. He wanted to call the new album "Bryan Adams Hasn't Heard of You Either."

What a FANTASTIC title! Of course, the record label rejected it so the less snarky "You Want It You Got It" became the title.

The lead single "Lonely Nights" peaked at number three on Billboard's Mainstream Rock Tracks chart. Since then he has sold nearly 86.5 million in equivalent album sales (physical and streamed). To put that into context, it is more than Justin Bieber and Drake!

I Share This Story For Two Reasons

First, it is a great example of tenacity and perseverance. He learned from his previous experience and came back stronger. He wrote the breakthrough record he hoped for. Critics praised him, audiences applauded him and radio embraced him. He reached a larger audience.

Secondly, he took the lack of recognition with humor and positive energy. Instead of giving the music industry the middle finger and taking a job at a fast food restaurant super sizing everything, he took it as an opportunity to grow and improve.

Failure is an opportunity for growth. You've heard it before but we don't always accept it or we choose to ignore it. The reality is, if you aren't failing, then you haven't tried hard enough. Einstein, Jobs, Musk, Oprah and the list goes on, failed. Multiple times.

Do you remember the Apple Newton? Of course not. It was probably one of Apple's greatest failures.

Creativity is about many ideas.

Iterate! People tend to give up too soon. We try something and if it doesn't seem creative enough, throw our hands up in the air. It's usually followed by the decision to get a job at the local hardware store or fast food restaurant because we are clearly not creative enough. Sound familiar?

Trial and error. I can honestly say that many of my best solutions sprung from a failed idea. It lead me on a path of further exploration.

Look at your failures objectively and decide if you should explore the idea more or simply ball up the piece of paper and try for a three-pointer into the garbage can across the room.

Does This Style Make me Look Phat?

The Futile Search For A "Style"

When I was fresh out of school and for the first few years of my career, I was chasing style. What was my "look?" How was I going to plant my flag in the design world and garner the acclaim that I felt I deserved? Youthful bravado that falsely inflates our chest and head. Look out world, I graduated at the top of my class! Guess what? Crickets. No one cared. And rightfully so. I had made some critical errors in my thoughts. Style won at school. But there wasn't the intense reality of clients and true deadlines. I was mistaking style for approach.

Don't get me wrong. I fully endorse looking at the design annuals, and searching through websites for inspiration. But that is a slippery slope. It will lead to intense, and I mean INTENSE Impostor Syndrome.

Let it Go Picasso, *This Ain't Fine Art.*

The game I hate playing most is Pictionary. Every time I get together with friends and someone wants to play it, I'll inevitably draw something, everyone will stop, look at it and ask "what is that, I thought you do this for a living?" Of course I don't play Pictionary for a living. My goal of sketching is to get ideas out quickly and effectively so I don't forget them. I don't spend hours refining and making them beautiful. The same goes for Pictionary.

Many of us come to this industry through a love of art. As kids we grew up drawing, cutting paper, finger painting as often as we could. We could spend hours…

Every birthday we were showered in new pencils, paper, sketch books, paint, etcetera. Our work proudly on display on the white-textured fridge held up with a magnetic red plastic letter.

As a design professional, you are using a portion of that talent to aid in the delivery of a message but it ends there. This work is not being framed, curated at a museum or even put on the fridge in our parents' house. The lifespan of a lot of our work is quite short, particularly in the digital space.

As a designer, you have a client who has an audience. Your job is to communicate to that audience, not just create something you like.

Everything you work on from the initial brainstorm sketches to the final product is about results. Our work is defined by analytics and ROI — not creative expression.

While this might feel like a downer to the part of you that wants to express yourself, understanding this will save you a whole lot of stress and anxiety.

Use this understanding to sketch ideas freely and doodle with abandon. The point is to get your ideas out early and quickly so you can do your job.

Use it to remember feedback on your work is not personal. None of this is about you.

Save the tortured artist tantrum for after hours.

A Lesson in Self-awareness
Let's call him David

I was fortunate to have first met "David" as a student of mine. Quiet. Sat at the back of class. He was also a "rocker". He dressed like an 18 year old Mick Jagger/Keith Richards. He would become an employee and eventually, a great friend.

As an employee, he was efficient, precise and immensely talented. Any time I would give him an annual report full of charts graphs and gridded layouts, he would excel. Without a doubt the best corporate designer I have come across. Still with the rock/punk persona he was definitely a study in contrast.

I remember a specific day when he was working on two annual reports and I felt bad. He was so talented but I had him doing production on this corporate work. I went over and assured him that I had a few creative projects in the wings waiting for him. His response floored me. Turns out he LOVED working on the annual reports with all the charts and graphs. It's what he wanted to work on. Taken aback, I asked why. He explained that he was in a band and loved to write music.

His job at the agency allowed him to work in the industry he chose and then go home and write music. The corporate work allowed him to be creative at home. He explained that if he was working on a logo or something with fewer parameters he would not have the energy or creativity to write music at night.

David taught me that self-awareness will bring you happiness and fulfillment.

"I am an awa[re]
creative, the [...]
society no lo[nger...]

"...d-winning ...ules of normal ...ger apply"

— Ben Day, protagonist in the short film *"Ben Day"*

SUCKcess

The Endless Search for Recognition

When I started in this career, I was obsessed with awards and trophies. I was constantly seeking recognition and validation through awards and admiration through colleagues.

All the wrong things.

Blue Ribbons and Bowling Trophies

Caked in dust and full of pictures of summer vacations, sports and birthday parties, the family album is a time capsule. They also contain ribbons, photos of awards ceremonies and trophies. Accomplishments and successes. We move forward in life and reminisce on those moments.

These days the dusty books are replaced by digital archives but the content has not changed. There is certainly an overabundance of awards. It seems like there is an award for everything. If you really want or need the recognition I am sure that you will find it. Most competitions don't care if you nominate yourself.

I have won a crap-load of awards for my work. So what, right? Exactly. What does it all mean? Ultimately, I'm sorry to say, nothing. It's true. At best, it will make you feel better for a day or two and it will make your mom proud. The trap is, awards have an expiry date. They are only good for a year, at most, and become redundant as time passes. Eventually they become a sad reminder that you haven't won anything recently.

Awards have an expiry date. They are only good for a year at most and become redundant as time passes. They become a sad reminder if you haven't won anything recently.

Expectations are like armpits; they make you sweat and eventually stink.

Early SUCKcess

My first encounter with the sting of success was at the age of ten. I wasn't particularly athletic, so sports trophies were out of my reach and my academic prowess was yet to present itself. So, when a Grade 5 Halloween costume contest at school was announced, I was going to nail it!

This was my opportunity to shine. Being artistically inclined and Star Wars obsessed, I spent all my spare time creating the greatest Darth Vader mask. It was awesome.

Papier-mâché was my chosen medium. A balloon, bowl of water and paste the infamous helmet came together in a fervor of newspaper strips and black paint. Problem was, I had forgotten about the rest of the costume, so in a last-minute panic I grabbed a garbage bag for a cape, put on black pants, t-shirt and a pair of tall black boots I found in the hall closet. Off I went to school. In my head, I had nailed it.

I was the best Darth Vader, in fact I was expecting a call from George Lucas asking me to consult on the next movie. Recess came and there I stood, a dark figure in a sea of princesses, off-green Hulks and tinfoil wrapped robots. The judges walked up and down assessing the store-bought or hand-made costumes until the announcement was made. I had won! Success, or so I thought. In the following days, I discovered that success was not what I had envisioned. Ridicule and mockery greeted me down every hall. WAIT! Where were the accolades? The adoration? Success was not what I expected. It sucked!

I had become the kid who showed up to schocl in his mother's leather boots and a garbage bag cape.

"I find your lack of faith in my costume disturbing."

Eventually Only Your Mother Will Care

Anytime I achieved "success," as defined by society or what I assumed success to be, it sucked. I hated it and I was miserable. Why?

It becomes added stress. Expectations from yourself, colleagues and clients will circle like vultures. What have you done lately? The potential sophomore slump or one hit wonder will haunt you.

Understand that awards are arbitrary and expensive. They are a reflection of the time, number of entries, judges and a myriad of other factors. Don't ever take them too seriously. They will eventually tarnish and end up in landfill.

Success isn't a trophy. It's personal growth and development. It's having a positive impact on other people's lives, even if only one person.

Defining Success

I'm not here to tell you what the definition of success is. I'm here to tell you that you need to define it for yourself.

Success doesn't have to be a Mercedes or that big house in the rich neighborhood or any of those trappings. But it can be. Again, that's up to you.

The important thing is to live by your own definition of success, not someone else's.

If you go after someone else's idea of success, you will likely not attain it and even if you do it will suck. Just as I found out.

So once you're sure what success is for you, go for it! Fill your boots! And celebrate living a genuine life, something that feels right for you, and that your definition of success means something to you. I would also consider re-evaluating your version of success if it involves hurting other people or crushing their values or idea of success.

When you reach your own defined level of personal success you will glow. Your energy will be contagious. THAT'S something worth working for.

The important thing is to live by your own definition of success, not someone else's.

Also, success doesn't have to be physical—a car, a house or any possession. Success can be education, learning a new skill or something you've always wanted to do. Maybe it's dance, photography or film making, or finally getting a painting done that you always wanted to do. That can all be defined as success. Success doesn't need to cost money or be public.

If we think about it, success is a word that means different things to different people. I had fallen into society's definition of success: the attainment of wealth, position, honors, or the like… blah blah blah…

SNORE! Maybe that was the problem, success seemed boring. Where do you go from there? You spend so much time trying to attain success, once you achieve it, the drive is gone. What's next? And by the way, success has a shelf life. A short one. That voice in your head will soon whisper in your ear, "Yeah, but what have you done lately?" That voice is an asshole and a major buzzkill.

Success should feel great, right? High fives, confetti canons and popped champagne! So, why was I unsatisfied? Well, aside from the lack of champagne and confetti canons, it just felt empty. I needed to understand "success".

Success to me became much simpler. It's the freedom to take my two sons out for dinner, drinks and a movie without worrying about my bank balance. It's about family.

If I knew there was always discretionary money available after paying for my living expenses, I had achieved a level of success. Something to celebrate! Maybe not popping bottles of overpriced champagne but grabbing an ice-cold beer from the fridge. Maybe I'll shake it up for the same effect?

You have to create your own definition of success. What do you want from life?

What is your champagne moment?

Think
Like an Olympian

Every now and then you receive surprising advice from the most unexpected sources.

This time, it was from my brother-in-law. I was floored when, after a few years of him dating my sister, I found out he is a former Olympian. WHAT?!?! Now, don't get me wrong, he's incredibly fit and I can totally picture him as a world-class athlete, but it caught me off guard —to say the least. And he didn't just compete in one Olympic Games but two! TWO!

I decided given his background he would be an excellent source of information. How do elite athletes mentally prepare to compete at an international level? What's the holy grail of self-awareness and mental preparedness? Maybe he'd have some of the answers I had been searching for.

So, at a family gathering, somewhere between "…pass the ham", and "…I just can't eat quinoa, it looks like worms," I seized the opportunity.

"How do you mentally prepare to compete in the Olympics? How do you deal with the fact that you are up against the top athletes from around the world?" Did he have a process or mindset I could use myself?

Is there a "zone"? I want to have a zone. How do I find my zone? What's the secret???

His answer wasn't what I expected at all.

"I don't think about the other competitors," he said dryly.

That was it.

The answer that I had been waiting for. The secret… Wait…

WHAT???

Where's the insider trick that only elite athletes know? Where's the magic?

But then he continued. "Their performance is something that I have no control over. I focus on beating my best time. I can control my pace, my rhythm, my breathing. I can't control theirs. If I beat my own personal best then I succeed. If it means a medal, great, but that's not the point."

This has stuck with me for many years. In the end, I did get the answer I was looking for—it's just not what I expected. It was better! I use it constantly and so should you. You can't control others or situations around you. Just you.

A Lesson in Self-worth
Let's call her Amanda

"Amanda", a fellow designer who works for a hospital, was down on herself for not being a great designer. It brought her stress and affected her work. More importantly, it was eroding her confidence and self-esteem. She felt that she did not measure up to other designers. Classic Impostor Syndrome and so wrong.

She confided with me that when she looked at other designers, she felt like a "hack". I asked her who she was comparing herself with. The designers she listed were internationally recognized. Industry "rock stars". Their clients were mainly museums, theaters, musicians and corporations with large budgets. I had to agree that their work was outstanding, however she didn't dig deep enough. To begin with, the work that she saw on their websites was limited. In fact, there may be only two or three pieces for any given year. Obviously, there is a lot of work that they are not showing. Work that pays the bills. I'm sure that if she only showed a few pieces of her work from any given year she would be surprised and proud of what she had created. Secondly, the work that they showed was highly artistic and bordered on fine arts and self-expression and did not communicate.

There is no way that their approach or aesthetic would work for a hospital. (I would argue that it didn't work for their clients either.) It's art and nothing more. What she creates is so much more and affects so many on a daily basis. Her graphics communicate information and deliver important messages. My point is, context is crucial and that is what we find when we dig deeper.

The Takeaway

Try not to compare your work to anyone. It is yours and yours alone. As I have said before, this is not self-expression but your approach is unique. It should be informed and appropriate to the subject matter, client and audience. Comparing it to work that is not in the same industry, audience or culture will not achieve anything except regret and Impostor Syndrome. Judge your work based on client feedback and audience engagement. That is the measure. Too often we compare our work to that of industry "rock stars" and that is not a fair comparison. I fully support being inspired by their work but not to compare it with. There is a big difference.

Where d

you get your ideas?

Birds, Bees and Ideas

"Where do your ideas come from"?, is probably one of the most common questions I get. And every time, it feels like that frightening day when a child asks their parents "where do babies come from?".

The answer can be awkward, anecdotal, scientific or a blabbering mess of ummms and welll... Basically it comes down to mindset, environment and, in some cases, patience.

Now patience isn't always a luxury we have, so let's explore some exercises to help you short-circuit the process when needed.

How does this make you feel?

The Curse
of Carte Blanche

Not a bad French horror film from the 60s, but just as terrifying. I like to call it 'Mad Designers Disease'.

The last spread was intentionally left blank. How did it make you feel? Anxious, excited or just annoyed that the printer made a mistake? Whatever it was, take a moment and think about it. You will feel one of two ways, anxious or excited.

Anxious

Fear of the blank page is real and we all face it sometimes but we don't have to. Some people think that insanity is trying the same thing over and over and expecting a new result. For me it's when there aren't any rules. This is the core of the blank page syndrome. In this case, blank describes your brain, not the paper. Let's face it, paper is quite happy to be blank. We're the ones that mess it up with doodles and sketches. We're paper's worst nightmare.

So, you have cracked open your sketchbook to a fresh blank piece of paper. Now what? Anxiety sets in, but it doesn't have to. You have everything you need to start. Begin by writing down relevant words and thoughts from the brief. If you have done your research, you will never have to fear the black page again.

Excited!

This is where you should be. Bliss! A page full of possibility. No rules, both figuratively and literally. The blank page is where we should always start our projects. They're easily filled with relevant words and thoughts from the brief. Once all of the exploration, doodles, distractions and tangents fill the page(s) you can start to eliminate, refine and finesse.

Ice cream, Lizards, and Procrast

...nation

For the rest of us, when confronted with the looming specter of a deadline, we always pray to whom or whatever, promising that we will NEVER do it again. We will follow a calendar. Organize our time better, blah, blah, blah… only to do it again. Why???

Well, it's the 'Lizard Brain' (limbic cortex is the fancy name for it). It's that part of the brain that loves trouble. It's lazy and obnoxious.

I put the Pro in procrastination. It's my super power. I want to make myself a cape but I never get around to it. If I can put it off, I will. I am really good at making myself busy with lots of unrelated and non-urgent tasks when a deadline looms.

Sound familiar?

Emails top my list of distractions. Reading them, writing them and even thinking about who I haven't emailed in a while. I follow that up with phone calls and then the obligatory desk tidying (admittedly, there is some social mediaing and doodling in there too). Soon enough, I'm sitting at an obscenely clean desk, emails done, cartoon animals doodled on my phone bill and no one left to call.

Then the stress hits. Shit! That task that I have put off is now facing me, head on. Like those boxing or MMA posters where the two contenders aggressively stare each other down—except my stare down isn't as intimidating. I feel threatened. Now I NEED to do it. Stress is now replaced with panic. The first four letters in the word DEADline are now screaming at me.

Basically, it feels good to put off a task we don't want to do. Instead we want to do something fun! Anything, really.

The lizard brain loves that. The dopamine courses through our brains and off we go day dreaming, netflixing, air-guitaring and ice cream eating. We're 12 again and it's glorious! Even for an hour or two. Then, like your parents returning home to witness your out of control house party, your adult returns. Voices yelling and fingers waving. Head down and bottom lip fully extended, you revert to reality.

There are those of us who thrive on the adrenaline rush of an impending deadline. You may be one of them. Let's call them "task masochists". They greet a ticking clock with the enthusiasm of a kid with an ice cream cone. These techniques are not for them.

How do we fix this? Let's explore two strategies, reward and risk.

The Trick with Treats

Deadlines are a reality, so why do we continually struggle with them? Time and again we put things off only to induce panic once again.

How do we fix this? Why not reverse this way of thinking where things get done AND keep the lizard happy? How about making a deal with yourself? Get that task done first and guarantee yourself a reward.

I have a friend who, along with her partner, put time aside where they both agree to do the unpleasant task(s) they have been putting off. When completed, they have ice cream. In her experience things get done quickly and sometimes they keep going.

Just make sure you have the treat ready when you are done. No cheating!

Risk *vs Reward*

Maybe you tried the ice cream reward strategy and it didn't work. You just ended up with a bowl full of guilt with a little on your shirt and you're still sitting on the couch.

It's time to put something on the line.

If you're like me, you might find risk more motivating. One of the greatest motivators is accountability.

Whether your goal is to mount an exhibit, write a book, perform a song or anything in between, establish the day you're going to do it and tell people. Now!

If you're procrastinating, create a little risk. Visualize that finish line. Make it real. Set an end date and tell people about it.

When you find yourself stalling, it helps to have others around to give you a little push.

Forgetting that your computer is a tool makes you the tool.

When you're looking for your idea, the last thing you should do is sit in front of your computer. Computers were not designed to create or solve problems like we are. Creativity is an inherent human ability. Computers require our input—we shouldn't be seeking theirs. This is completely backwards if you are in the creative industry. Rethink how you approach your problem-solving and communication. If you are going straight to the computer then you are thinking execution and not creation.

Trust your brain and use the computer to enhance your work.

> "When you hear hoof-beats, think of horses not zebras."
>
> — Dr. Theodore Woodward

Nope. No zebras here.

Stop Looking for Zebras

Zebras? Let me explain.

First year medical interns are taught this quote from Dr. Theodore Woodward. It is of particular importance for ER interns when diagnosing a patient. Essentially, it explains if someone presents with stomach pains, for example, don't automatically assume they have Crimean-Congo Hemorrhagic Fever. They simply may have eaten some bad sushi.

The same principle can easily be applied to the creative industry and the pressure you put on yourself to come up with incredible ideas. I spent so many years looking for zebras.

What are our zebras? They are that elusive fully original idea. The one concept that will win all of the awards and envy of everyone in the industry. The one where I'd be called up on stage to accept the funky metal trophy then thank my team, clients, mother, babysitter and teachers. I was under the delusion, like a lot of us, that the answer to creativity is in the original, the obscure and the truly unique.

There were many sleepless nights, lots of foul language and collateral damage (broken pencils, crumpled paper, uncrumpled paper…) as I'd try to come up with that winning idea.

It was a frustrating cycle of looking for, and failing to find that perfect idea. The zebra.

Many designers fall into this trap where no idea is ever good enough. Not unique enough.

The truth is, we are over-complicating things. Over-thinking and (in my case), over caffeinating.

Take a breath. Relax.

You are staring at a herd of horses looking for a zebra. Unless you are at the zoo or in Africa, you ain't gonna spot one. A can of black paint and a cooperative white horse won't do it either.

We spend far too much time over-complicating and over-thinking when confronted by a new project.

Percolation
is Not Just for Coffee.

The reason you will suddenly have an idea in the shower or at night and any other inconvenient time, is processing or percolating. Some refer to it as "sleeping on it". Basically, ideas don't just pop into your head. There is no divine intervention or idea fairy. Ideas come because of a process. When you read, investigate, and research, you prime your brain. It happens, or should, before you execute. This process will elicit words, images and thoughts. When you are at ease, like in the shower, your ideas will come. Why? Because they have peculated. Now, get them down on paper and try not to get soap in your eyes.

The Permission Principle

Do you ever feel like you're wasting time when you stop to sketch, ideate, or even think in the middle of a workday?

Have you ever felt guilty, like you should get back to actual "work"? You feel a presence looking over your shoulder, judging you.

If so, you need to stop that thinking right away.

The feeling of guilt comes from an antiquated definition of what "work" is. It's based on the idea that you need to be producing something at all hours of the day to be valuable, and if you don't, you're unproductive and lazy.

The reality is anything but.

I'm sure you have felt exhausted after a day or even a few hours of creative problem-solving? I have, and rightfully so. Coming up with impactful ideas IS work. It takes time and it takes energy.

Stop beating yourself up. You need to block off periods of creative thinking. It's not only productive but necessary.

It will make the execution phase more productive and will actually save time. Don't fall into the trap of feeling guilty.

Give yourself permission to carve out time to be creative.

Why? No one else will unless you bring it up.

If you work in an environment that supports this or even encourages it, don't take that for granted. Appreciate it and the leadership that empowers you. If not, start the conversation. No one will do it unless they know it is an issue. Advocate for yourself, your time and your creativity.

Give yourself permission to carve out time in your day to be creative.

Turn That Racket Off!

Silent contemplation and reflection has become a rare occurrence in our daily routine. The number of hours either watching television or in front of a computer/smartphone has dramatically increased at the expense of "quiet time". Even in bed we have our phones, laptops or tablets when we should be focusing on shutting ourselves down.

There should be a time in our day for reflection, calm and peace. I remember telling my sons, when they were young, that it was quiet time. They would throw themselves to the ground in frustration yelling "NO…NO …NOT QUIET TIME!" in between sobs. All I could think about at the time was that I would pay GOOD MONEY to have some quiet time!

Now there are a lot of you out there who enjoy yoga or hour-long meditations, which is excellent, but I am not suggesting you start there.

With all of the messages inundating us, the first step is to get comfortable with the quiet. It may sound simple and rudimentary, but it isn't easy.

A great way to start is to do it right before you go to sleep. This is where most of my "noise" is. That's when my mind starts to think about the day's events, new ideas and that jerk who cut me off in traffic.

That's when it's time to turn it off.

Start by focusing on your breathing. Tune out the creaks and cracks of your bedroom, the ambient noise from outside or upstairs and simply focus on your quiet breaths, in and out.

Get comfortable with quiet

It will be hard at first so don't give up. Breathe. In and out. Even if only for a couple of minutes.

This will help in so many ways but for now it will help quiet the noise and help you fall asleep more quickly. This is the basis for basic meditation. Start to build on it. Every time your mind wanders to what's for dinner, breathe. And again and again. It takes practice but the payoff is huge.

Another change that you can make is the next time you get home and want to automatically throw on the television or music, stop and take a moment. Don't turn anything on. Take off your jacket and shoes. Make sure your keys are ready for the morning on the entrance table or shelf. Sit on the coziest chair that you have and take a few deep breaths. If you don't have a comfy chair, get up, put on your jacket and shoes, grab your keys and go get one! Everyone needs a comfy chair.

Silence and reflection are gifts. You deserve them. The good news is that they're free! The alternative is to live in the racket. And that can cost a lot!

Creating in a Vacuum is for Dyson

It's been my experience, throughout my career, that the best work comes from collaboration. Always. You are working for a client with an audience. Working alone doesn't provide the multiple thoughts, opinions and discussions that mass communication demands. Even if the client is yourself.

So, clean off your desk. Put the cat on the floor and get ready to collaborate. As I said, your work will be so much better.

Collaboration
is the Key to Great Work

With so many teams working remotely, isolation has become a reality for most designers and content creators. Who wants to get on a video call to brainstorm when you could just get it done on your own (and stay in your PJs)?

Here are some things to keep in mind to get the most out of being inclusive in your process.

Step 1

Identify your team and or collaborators.

Create a go to list of trusted collaborators. This may be the people on your team, clients or people you've worked with before and admire. Not poker buddies, the Starbucks barista or your mom.

When possible, this list should also include a sample of the intended audience, but keep this list small.

Step 2

Be clear about what you want from them.

Be clear about what you want when sending your work to your collaborators. What would be helpful? Ask for specific feedback, editing or design input. Make it clear what parts you want feedback on and what you're looking to achieve.

When possible, show concepts in black and white. People automatically shift into personal preference when something is presented in color. Black and white presentations ensure the focus is on the message, concept and approach.

Make it clear you're not simply looking to know which one they like. You need to know their "why".

Step 3

Apply selected feedback and refine your work.

Review all the feedback from your collaborators, but be careful about applying it. It's easy to feel overwhelmed by a lot of feedback and all of it won't be positive. Take it with a grain of salt, like a good margarita.

Look for the commonalities and pieces that resonate and apply that. If you apply every single person's feedback your work can end up generic when you need strong and concise. It can also feed Impostor Syndrome.

Selectively apply the feedback that makes sense. The more you do it, the more confident you'll feel about it.

You are your ow[n]
Don't expect oth[ers]
respect you if yo[u don't respect]
yourself. Stop an[d listen]
to how you spea[k]
about your achie[vements]

n worst enemy.

er people to

u don't respect

d pay attention

к to others

ements.

Learn a New Language: Confidence

Self-deprecation is a slippery slope. It is steeped in language. When we constantly, and usually jokingly, self-deprecate we not only hurt ourselves but give permission to others to do the same. So many people use this, me included, as a form of humor but its roots run deeper. It is about self-confidence and self-worth. It's a defense mechanism. Instead of opening ourselves up to criticism we take the initiative and do it before someone else can.

Not to sound like your grade four teacher with eyes firmly fixed on you, slightly peering above thick rimmed glasses, but watch your language! I mean it! Now, before you get bent out of shape or excited, this post is not about profanity. It's about the words we use in our everyday life, although admittedly, some of them have four letters.

You see, our brain is incredibly powerful. It rules everything, good and bad. We also know that repetition is a powerful tool for memory and learning. That's why the words or language that we use daily are so important. The way we describe ourselves, finances and our job. It's something that we rarely pay attention to because it becomes a habit. This is where a lot of us begin and strengthen our self-destructive patterns. In my book *The Frankenstein Condition*, I describe it as the monster we create. Much like Victor Frankenstein, we create our monsters from pieces of the people around us.

People we admire, whether through social media or real life: celebrities, family and friends. Language is the thread that we use to stitch our monster together.

We do this in conversation with others and through repetition begin to believe it ourselves. We say things like "I'm always late" or "I'm really lazy" or "cook? I can't even boil an egg." These seem rather innocuous but when repeated we begin to believe them. You will always be late, lazy and a horrible cook because you have accepted it. Reality is made through language.

Don't dismiss or diminish them. "That shirt looks great!"… "This old thing… I got it for 5 bucks on sale". Change that to "Thanks!" Be appreciative and positive. Accept compliments.

Pay attention to the words that you use or associate with the important things in life. It's amazing how much you can change your world with just words. It's something you can do right away and it will have a profound impact on your happiness and the people around you. And don't forget to mind your P's and Q's!

It's confidence not ego.

Don't diminish yourself.

Coulda, shoulda, kinda, sort of… It weakens your position and authority. You have a place at the table. You are the expert.

Speak with intent and purpose.

Blah, blah, blah.

Keep to the point and save the industry lingo for speaking with industry professionals, not clients or colleagues. Think about your audience. Speak in their language. Use business terms and language appropriate to the presentation like process, outcome, ROI etcetera. Make it results-focused and not subjective.

Be inclusive. Always.

When presenting concepts or designs use words like we, together, us and use people's names in presentations. "Dave, you mentioned that we should really focus on the untapped cat market so we incorporated…" They are less likely to poke holes in your design if they feel like they were part of the process.

Jargony Jargon

There is nothing more irritating than trying to understand what a company does when described using jargon. It's like trying to understand your tax return line by line or the terms of agreement for the latest app. Nope. We really should understand those things but they are clearly, or unclearly, written by people who understand them but not how to write in English.

As communicators, we are regularly faced with dense verbose content written by someone in-house and edited by someone in HR. In the end you aren't sure if you have applied for a job or read instructions on how to disarm a bomb. We are good at simplifying ideas and articulating a company's value—after all we are communicators.

Present the Concept and Pass the Potatoes

Many of us struggle when it comes to presenting concepts. After all of the hair pulling, teeth gnashing and head banging, we finally arrived at a solution for the client. It is tight, on strategy and dynamite. Or so we think. But what about the client? What will they think? Anxiety rounds the corner and hits you at full force. Shit... The same can be said for presenting a portfolio or a job interview. The same principles apply.

Presentation Strategies

This is gonna hurt, so sit down.

While you might have the greatest solution possible, the presentation is impeccable, the strategy is sound, thinking about it makes the hair on the back of your neck perk up—this can all fall apart if its not presented properly. So many great ideas die in the presentation. While the majority of us hate presenting the idea, it's this stage that will make or break the client's acceptance. The key to this is to strip all emotion and back it up with facts and data.

What if you are suddenly presenting it to a committee or board? This is where great ideas go to die. As the quote goes "A camel is a horse designed by committee". I think it is more like a duck-billed platypus. All that to say, your great idea will not proceed without the buy in of the audience. Again, this is not fine art, but the committee usually treats it like that. They will use words like "I don't like blue", etc... without a great guide and moderator, this will not go well.

If you go in prepared and confident, you will succeed.

Seriously, who looks forward to making a presentation? For most of us, it's all we can do not to throw up or pass out.

Presentations with all the fixin's

So, how do you present to a group or committee and not throw up? The first step is to prepare. Going into the meeting confident involves having a professional presentation, so don't underestimate the value of practicing, reviewing and for the love of puppies, spell check! I wouldn't say it if I hadn't seen it or, gulp, done it myself. These are things you are in control of.

Now let's look at something you are not always in control of—your audience. I have been in many situations where I thought I was presenting to one or two people and walked into a room full of people. Did I miss a memo? Were they giving out invitations at Starbucks? Did I accidentally walk into a birthday party? Whatever the reason is, you have to deal with it and it can take the wind out of you. Now you see how important it is to prepare your material. You will lean heavily on the confidence that you are prepared and the work is on strategy. Now, after you get over the fact that there is no cake, let's look at who may be in attendance and how to deal with them.

We have all heard the "think of everyone in their underwear" advice to lessen the stress but honestly… underwear? For me it makes more sense to think of presentations as a family dinner.

The key to a successful presentation lies in your understanding that not all attendees are created equal. Most designers focus entirely on the work being presented and not the "room". Your attendees are as much a part of a presentation's success as the work itself. Sad to say but true. Just like serving dinner to a table full of hungry guests, there is one meal for everyone but not everyone is looking for the same thing. Here is an example of what I mean. It may be extreme and thankfully not all meetings are like this. That said, ensuring that your presentation has a little for everyone, just like a good meal, everyone will leave satisfied.

The table is set. After hours of preparation, combining the right ingredients and applying your best techniques the meal is ready and one by one the guests arrive. (It's important to note that unlike most meals, you may enter a room or video conference and there are suddenly more people than you expected or were told would be in attendance.)

Let's take a look at who came for dinner.

The Parents
(AKA the Client, Marketing Manager)

They called the meeting. They are trying to make sure order is kept. They want everything to be perfect and go smoothly.

How to deal with them
You are their ally here. You are the manifestation of their project and decision making so you need to make them look good. A professional, well thought out presentation is what they want. They also want to be acknowledged for their participation in the process. You didn't work in a vacuum (see what I did there). It will also build credibility for you and your work if they were an active participant in the process.

Job titles: The direct client, Marketing Manager, VP of Marketing, Account Manager

Aunt Edna
(AKA the CFO, COO, or Procurement)

Super picky. Food must not touch. Focuses on portions, ratios and wonders why Uncle Fred got more potatoes than she did. They are detail oriented and will focus on small errors and ask for clarification. Many times. They can be budget, data or information source focused and will interrupt for clarification.

How to deal with them
Always begin your presentation with the statement that questions are welcome after the presentation. You don't want to interrupt your pace and momentum. If they do interrupt, simply thank them for their question and you will address it after all of your material has been presented. Have your sources and data in the presentation to support what you are presenting. Keep this to a minimum though. Too much data/detail can rob a great concept presentation of its passion and impact. Use this data as punctuation after presenting a concept or to introduce it to defuse any potential questions.

Job titles: CFO, COO, some entrepreneurs/business owners, investors, lawyers and accountants or procurement.

Uncle Fred
(AKA the CEO, Owner)

Meat eater. They are the "get to the point". Appetizers, sides and salads are frustrating and distractions to the main course. They are only interested in meat.

How to deal with them
Eye contact works very well with this attendee. They will get frustrated with too much "fluff" so try to minimize it. This isn't a romance novel. Acknowledging them with eye contact will defuse this as they will be aware that you see them and that the meat is coming. If you can, call them out for information they may have provided or guidance. You are identifying that you are addressing their pain point. They are the ones on a road trip that don't want to look at a map, but will ask "are we there yet"?

Job titles: CEO, entrepreneurs/business owners

The Kids
(AKA Disgruntled Staff)

The kids are there because they must be there, but really don't want to be. And they are not paying attention whatsoever. They just want it to be over so that they can leave the table. Will eat quickly and get fidgety. Their attitude can have nothing to do with you or the presentation, but they will suck the energy out of the room.

How to deal with them
Well designed slides and humor. A dynamic presentation with colorful slides and images presented with passion will keep their interest. Eye contact is also effective.

Job titles: Interns, support staff, staff who have been told to attend the meeting

Random Pets

Unlike the kids, pets want to be there but not for good reasons. They are there to stir shit and have a free meal. These distractions randomly show up and voice their joy, displeasure or distress with what is happening outside the window. They invite themselves to the meeting. This can happen with large corporations and organizations. A meeting invite is sent out, it is placed on the calendar or the organizer/client is afraid of leaving anyone out. This guest has not been properly briefed on the project but possesses some corporate knowledge and a lot of attitude. They like having their names on the meeting notes as contributing regardless of value.

How to deal with them
These attendees need to know who is in charge. Your posture, tone of voice and eye contact will defuse this situation. Ask them questions while presenting. Involve them on your terms, not theirs.

Job titles: Anyone really. They can come from any department. The difference being if they come from management, they will command/demand a voice and people will listen. They may not agree but will smile and nod.

Like a great meal, make sure your presentation has a little something for everyone. You want them to leave the table satisfied.

now what?

It's the best time to be in the creative field, but it takes work.

Well, fellow rabble rousers and malcontents, it's time to get to work! Our time is now! It's not the meek who will inherit the earth. It's the disruptors.

In my opinion, it's the best time to be in the creative field and I hope that I have given you some tools or insights that will propel you forward. That said, it did not come easy for many of us and it is not simply being handed to us either.

The best way to conclude this book is to share my favorite quote on the next page. It is posted in my office as a constant reminder. If I had the courage, I would have it tattooed on me. Hmmm...

"Twenty years from now you will be more disappointed by the things you didn't do than by the ones you did do."

— Mark Twain

(This)
Robert Smith

His mother will tell you that he has always been a talented boy with an incredible imagination, always drawing or writing stories. His teachers would say the same but didn't share her enthusiasm. Not much has changed these days, thankfully. The difference is, he now applies those skills to help clients build confidence, rediscover their passion and experience a new level of energy in what they do.

Father of two sons, he finds them endlessly inspiring and a joy to be around.

Professionally he is a writer, internationally recognized creative director, agency owner, and educator. This is his second book and as you read this, a third is well on its way.

He currently coaches, educates and speaks to groups on the topic of creativity and living a life of passion. He also has a disdain for writing in the third person.

Wait, let's keep the conversation going...

We need to talk.

Let's face it, staying motivated isn't always easy! Whether you're a marketer, designer, writer or other professional in the creative industry, we can all use an inspirational jolt - and I don't mean coffee! This book is the first step of your new journey.

That's why I created Think Smith!

Looking for inspiration, guidance, or a kick in the creative ass to get you to that next stage? I help teams and individuals discover their creative potential through:

- Workshops
- One-on-one coaching
- Public speaking
- Consultation

Reach out and let's chat!

think-smith.com

www.ingramcontent.com/pod-product-compliance
Lightning Source LLC
Chambersburg PA
CBHW042114100526
44587CB00025B/4050